THE LITTLE
CAT CARE
Book

ELIZABETH MARTYN
DAVID TAYLOR
Photography by Jane Burton

DK

DORLING KINDERSLEY
London · New York · Stuttgart

DK

A DORLING KINDERSLEY BOOK

EDITOR Jane Mason
ART EDITOR Lee Griffiths
MANAGING EDITOR Krystyna Mayer
MANAGING ART EDITOR Derek Coombes
PRODUCTION Hilary Stephens

First published in Great Britain in 1991 by
Dorling Kindersley Limited, 9 Henrietta Street, London WC2E 8PS

A CIP catalogue record for this book is available
from the British Library

ISBN 0-86318-667-X

Reproduced by Colourscan, Singapore
Printed and bound in Hong Kong by Imago

CONTENTS

HAPPY CATS
PAMPERED CATS 10-11
FAMOUS CATS 12-13
BODY LANGUAGE 14-17
THE CAT FOR YOUR LIFESTYLE 18-19

HEALTHY CATS
CHOOSING A CAT OR KITTEN 22-23
KITTEN CARE 24-27
GROOMING YOUR CAT 28-37

TREATS FOR YOUR CAT
SENSUOUS DELIGHTS 40-41
GAMES AND PLAY 42-43
TREATS TO EAT AND MENUS 44-47

CAT FACTS
MY CAT'S HEALTH AND HISTORY 50-51
CAT STARS 52-55
A-Z OF HEALTH AND SAFETY 56-59

INDEX AND ACKNOWLEDGMENTS 60-61

HAPPY

Cats

*Body language, vocal
clues, and everyday
behaviour provide
valuable insights into
your cat's feelings.*

PAMPERED CATS

Throughout history, tradition has decreed that cats be a pampered, even venerated, species.

The tradition of treating cats lavishly began with the ancient Egyptians. A magnificent, red granite temple was built on the banks of the Nile River, and dedicated to Bastet, the ruling cat goddess. Cats inspired similar respect in Japan, where they were declared sacred around AD1000. For centuries cats were kept in the lap of luxury.

CARING FOR CATS
At the death of a beloved Egyptian domestic cat, the family shaved off their eyebrows as a sign of deep mourning. After an elaborate funeral, those cats belonging to especially wealthy owners were buried in jewelled caskets, with a generous supply of mummified rats and mice for nourishment in the afterworld.

The Prophet Mohammed cut off the sleeve of his robe rather than disturb his sleeping cat. Missionary Albert Schweitzer, who was left-handed, would write laboriously with his right hand in order not to waken his pet, Sizi, who so liked to curl up for a nap in the crook of his left arm. Sir Isaac Newton, famous pioneer of the sciences, is also credited with the invention of the cat door or cat flap. He cut two holes, one for his favourite cat and another, smaller one, for her litter of young kittens.

CLASSY CATS
Memorable examples of top cats are Hamlet, resident of the Algonquin Hotel in New York;

Left: Bathtime babies
Above: Mischief with the hatbox
Right: An Egyptian lady mourns her pet cat

or royal cats such as White Heather, Queen Victoria's pretty Persian. The Earl of Chesterfield left generous pensions to his cats when he died in 1773. Lucky cats in America and Britain have inherited up to £2 million.

FAMOUS CATS

Cats have been the chosen companions to generations
of the great and the good, the rich and the famous.

Their languorous elegance
delights artists, their discretion
appeals to politicians, and their
totally uninhibited behaviour
inspires writers. American
Presidents and British Prime
Ministers have
shared a great
affection for cats.

CATS IN POLITICS
Jock, Winston
Churchill's ginger
cat, slept on his
master's bed;
later, Nemu the
Siamese moved
into No. 10 with
Harold Wilson.
Wilberforce was
well known as
cat-in-residence
at Downing Street under four
Prime Ministers. Policemen on
duty outside No. 10 rang the
doorbell when Wilberforce
wanted to go in. The Roosevelt
family were cat-lovers. Slippers,
one White House resident, was

known to appear at many state
occasions. Another, Tom Quartz,
had his own biography written.

CATS IN LITERATURE
Many a famous writer has been
grateful for the
companionship
of a faithful cat.
Edgar Allen Poe
worked best with
his cat perched
on his shoulder.
Amazingly, Ernest
Hemingway did
complete one of
his novels in the
company of no
less than 34 cats.
Charles Dickens
often gave cats
bit parts in his
novels. He owned a white cat
called William, whose party trick
was snuffing out the candle with
his paw. The Bronte sisters, who
lived in an isolated Yorkshire
parsonage, enjoyed the company
of cats, and wrote sadly to close

Left: Actress Hayley Mills and contented feline friend
Right:Humphrey, currently in residence at No. 10 Downing Street
Below: Space cat Jones with Sigourney Weaver

friends to pass on the news when one very much-loved pet, called Tiger, died.

CATS IN THE MOVIES

Cats, as sensuous or sinister symbols, have made memorable appearances in films as diverse as *Breakfast at Tiffany's*, *The Incredible Journey*, *La Dolce Vita*, *Diamonds are Forever* (which features Solomon, an unblinking white chinchilla), and *Alien*. But perhaps the best recent celebration of cats has been Andrew Lloyd Webber's smash hit musical, *Cats*.

IS YOUR CAT HAPPY?

Your cat has an infinite variety of ways to tell you when all's right in the feline world. Ears pricked up and held forward show that your cat is alert and interested in what's going on. Whiskers pointing out to the sides of the face, neither bunched nor fanned out, mean puss is feeling calm and comfortable. A straight tail raised aloft is a way of saying "Hello". A quick flip of the tail tip is another greeting sign.

TRUSTING FRIEND
A confident cat rolls over, displaying his tummy. A cat who is less sure flops down at your feet to invite a stroke.

PERFECT PLEASURE
Purring is the ultimate expression of delight. The louder the purr, the happier the cat.

LITTLE GESTURES

Rubbing around your legs is a reminder that it's feeding time. Your cat is also marking you as feline property, using scent glands beneath the chin and forehead.

WONDERFUL WELCOME

A little-hop, with both front paws raised a few inches from the ground, sometimes accompanied by a little chirping cry, is an affectionate greeting used by cats pleased to see their owners.

FOND MEMORIES

When your cat leaps on to your lap and tramples your thighs with insistent paws, she is remembering the blissful days of kittenhood. Tiny kittens pummel their mother's belly to stimulate the flow of milk, and this habit is often retained in adult life.

IS YOUR CAT UNHAPPY?

If your cat is frightened or angry, all the clues are there to see. The pupils are enlarged, the ears held flat against the head, and the tail beats on the ground.

SOUNDS OF PROTEST

A high-pitched mew given by kittens is their only way of telling their mother that they are lost, cold, or frightened. The mew gets louder and more strident if the kitten is coming off

worse in a battle with one of his siblings. Adult cats use a short, high-pitched "miaow" to tell you that something is wrong. This is the cry you will hear when your cat has got herself shut in a room and wants to be freed at once. A cat who is feeling puzzled and unhappy gives a couple of quick tongue flicks over the lips. This is often the response to a particularly irritating noise.

FELINE ENIGMA

Ears, eyes, and whiskers are the chief indicators of a cat's mood. From the most usual neutral expression in the main picture, the cat's face may change to reveal a range of emotions from extreme fear to absolute comfort.

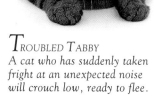

ATTACK ALERT

Most owners have seen their pet come face to face with the neighbourhood bully on the garden wall. The cat's ears turn back, and the head sways from side to side, with eyes fixed on the enemy. The whiskers fan out tensely, showing that action is imminent. The cat arches his back, and a band of fur stands up along his spine.

TROUBLED TABBY

A cat who has suddenly taken fright at an unexpected noise will crouch low, ready to flee.

ANXIOUS MOMENTS

Fur standing on end and ears flicked back show that this young cat is getting worried. Her tail is looped into the classic "witch's cat" position.

WATCHING AND WAITING

A cat poised with front legs straight and back legs bent is expressing uncertainty about what to do next. If the forelegs are also bent, and the cat is crouching, there's no doubt that danger is just around the corner. Rapid twitching of the ears is a sure sign of a cat who's feeling a trifle nervous. Watch your cat's ears next time you have to tick him off.

THE CAT FOR YOUR LIFESTYLE

Selecting the right cat to share your life isn't just a matter of picking the most appealing kitten in the litter. First you must decide what kind of cat would fit best into your world. Do you want an indoor cat, or will your new friend be free to roam? How much time can you spend with your cat – if the answer is very little, why not get two cats, as companions for each other. And can you cope with a kitten, or would an adult be a better choice?

THE PERFECT PET

As a very general rule, pedigree longhaired cats tend to be more placid by nature, and happier to stay at home than pedigree shorthaired, and particularly Oriental, breeds. However, you must have the time to spend on grooming. Some Oriental cats, like the Siamese and Burmese, crave company even though they also need freedom. Kittens need extra care and can be very demanding. Neutered males and females are equally sociable.

ALL-ROUND WINNER
The domestic non-pedigree is a robust cat, who adapts well to the rigours of family life.

CHARISMATIC CAT
Choose a regal Abyssinian for its boundless energy and superb good looks.

FRIENDLY GIANT
The tolerant and affectionate Maine Coon grows to a most impressive size.

HEALTHY
Cats

*All you need to know
about health, fitness, and
grooming to keep your
cat up to scratch.*

CHOOSING A CAT OR KITTEN

When you come to choose a cat or kitten, there are lots of important questions to bear in mind, from coat and colour, to behaviour and breed.

KITTEN OR CAT?

First decide whether you want a kitten or an adult cat. For the first couple of months, kittens need three meals a day and as much time as you can give them. Kittens are boisterous, so opt for a more sedate, older cat if you have a lot of treasures, or furniture that won't stand up to rough treatment. Before you bring your new cat home, make sure that a kitten has been given essential vaccinations, and that adults are up to date on boosters and have been neutered, unless you want to breed them, of course.

CHARACTER CAT
This young adult cat is alert, bright-eyed, and healthy.

The best place to get a cat or kitten is from someone you know, through a humane society, or from a breeder. Here's what to look for:

1 *Kittens should be playful and active. Encourage an older cat to jump or run to show that movement is easy.*

2 *Eyes should be bright, teeth sound, ears and nose clean. There should be no sign of an upset stomach.*

3 *The coat should be glossy and well cared for. Ruffle the fur backwards, to search for tell-tale black specks left by fleas.*

4 *Choose a cat that is inquisitive, and responds happily to being stroked and handled.*

5 *Longhairs demand time and patience for daily grooming sessions. Think carefully before making this commitment!*

*R*AGDOLL CHARMER
This little kitten displays the gentle demeanour that makes the breed so sought after.

*F*LUFFY FRIEND
Often docile by nature, longhairs are loyal and loving companions.

KITTEN CARE

Moving into a new home is a big adventure for a little
kitten, and one that should not be undertaken until
puss is at least eight to ten weeks old.

First Things First

Before you bring your kitten
home, make a few preparations.
Kittens need a bed of their
own, lined with a warm,
washable blanket, personal
bowls for food and water and,
of course, a litter tray.

Lessons for Life

Give your kitten lots of
affection. Welcome her on to
your lap, and pick her up if she
cries for attention. Don't be
too soft though. It's never too
soon to start teaching that
"No" definitely means "NO!"

Help!

*Ginger is only six weeks
old when she first meets
a young pup – and she is
just a bit scared.*

BEST FRIENDS
*Soon puppy and kitten
are playing together
happily. Careful early
introductions make for
lasting friendships.*

TRAINING TECHNIQUES

How much you can train your cat to do, depends on how willing your cat is to be trained! To achieve the best results, start early, and be patient but persistent.

Leading the Way

Many cats are happy to walk on a lead. Start training in kittenhood, letting your cat get used to wearing the lead without you holding it. Give short training sessions, indoors at first. Don't drag at the lead: use gentle encouragement with lots of reassuring words. Only venture outside when your cat is completely used to walking with you.

Walkies!

Siamese and other Oriental cats enjoy walking on a lead.

IN AND OUT
*If you fit a cat door for your pet,
make sure that you choose one
that has a lock or closure for
night-time security.*

FELINE FREEDOM
Both cats and owners
appreciate the advantages of a
cat flap, which allows your pet
to come and go freely. Some
cats take to them immediately,
while others find them puzzling
and even frightening. If your
cat seems confused, try
propping the flap open for a day
or two, so that she gets used to
hopping through the gap. Then
try closing the flap and calling
her name, or rattling a food
bowl from the other side as an
extra incentive. Cats are clever
creatures and soon
work out just
what to do.

LITTER LESSONS
Cats are instinctively clean and
quickly learn to use a litter
tray, which should always be
kept in the same place to avoid
mistakes and confusion.
Keep the tray clean and clear
up any mishaps with mild
bleach, *never* ammonia.

GOOD HABITS
*Pop your kitten into the
tray after meals. In a day
or two she will know the routine.*

COAT CARE

There's no getting away from it, daily grooming is vital for many cats. Make it a pleasure rather than a chore – your cat will thoroughly enjoy your undivided attention and you'll be rewarded by the glorious sight of your glamorous pet.

*L*ONGHAIRED *L*OVELY
A contented cat, freshly groomed to fluffy perfection.

*T*ANGLE *F*REE
Work methodically to remove knots. If your cat roams outside, you will probably find burrs and bits of twig caught up in the coat.

Essential Equipment

A bristle brush is kind to the coat and good for all-over brushing. Use a wire slicker brush to work through the length of the fur. Combs with wide and narrow teeth are useful for teasing out knots and tangles. Cotton-wool buds come in handy for cleaning the ears, but pads are safer when cleansing around the eyes. A soft toothbrush is ideal for gently teasing out the fur around the face and on the chest and legs. A soft cloth is often used for polishing the coats of shorthaired cats.

GROOMING SHORTHAIRS

Shorthaired cats make a good job of grooming themselves, but to keep them in top condition, they need regular brush-and-comb sessions to keep their coats glossy, smooth, and absolutely free of tangles.

Warning Signs

Black specks in the coat mean fleas. To check, wipe them on a moist tissue – if they are flea droppings they will leave a dark red smudge of blood. Treat your cat with a powder or spray.

Grooming Guide

1 Use a metal comb with fine teeth to work through the fur, starting from the head.

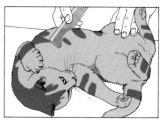

2 Now turn your cat over and gently comb the fur on the underside and chest.

AROUND THE EYES

Your cat's eyes should be bright and clear. Any discharge or inflammation may indicate a health problem. To remove unsightly "tear stains", wipe around the eyes with moist cotton wool.

CARING FOR CLAWS

Claws don't often become caked with dirt, but if they do, you can clean them using damp cotton wool. Trimming claws is tricky. Ask your vet to show you how to do it safely.

3 With a rubber brush, smooth the fur, working in the direction of growth.

4 Use a soft cloth, or a scrap of silk or velvet, to give a rich, glossy sheen to the coat.

GROOMING LONGHAIRS

Keep your longhaired cat looking absolutely
immaculate with thorough daily grooming.
Your cat will love the
attention, and you'll
be rewarded by a
vision of feline
splendour.

*T*OOTH CARE
*Keep a check on teeth and
gums. If necessary, the
teeth can be cleaned with a
soft brush and salt water.*

*G*ROOMING GUIDE

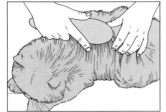

1 *Use a bristle brush to lift
   the fur all over the body
and to remove any loose hair.*

2 *Next, brush thoroughly up
   and down, remembering to
include tummy and tail.*

FABULOUS FUR

This Maine Coon steps out regally, showing finely feathered paws and a proudly plumed tail.

EYES AND EARS

Delicate areas need special care. Use moistened cotton wool to wipe away "tear stains" around the eyes. Use a damp cotton-wool bud to cleanse the outer ear gently – but don't probe too deep.

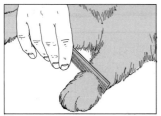

3 Use a comb to work gently at any stubborn tangles or knots in the luxuriant fur.

4 Finally, fluff up the fur around the face with a toothbrush for a pretty ruff.

PRIZEWINNERS

Is your cat champion material? There are numerous classes in which prizes are awarded in shows held every year. Non-pedigrees can enter too, and may win on the strength of charm and personality.

SHOW TIME

Don't subject a timid cat to the rigours of the show-ring, even if you think you own the most beautiful specimen ever born. Show cats are handled during judging and must feel perfectly at ease when being picked up and examined by total strangers. Your cat must put up with inquisitive human faces peering into the pen – heaven for an extrovert Siamese, but purgatory for a timorous Russian Blue.

PEAK CONDITION

Longhaired cats should have the fur fluffed out on body and face for showing purposes.

WELL PREPARED

Regular grooming in the weeks
leading up to the show, plus a
good and varied diet, will ensure
that puss is in top form on the
day. Make sure that vaccinations
are up-to-date in good time,
otherwise your cat will not be
allowed to compete.

POINT SCORES

Entrants must match
up to the standard set
for their breed,
covering condition;
texture and colour
of coat; shape of
the body, head,
and tail; and
shape and colour
of the eyes.

CAT ACCESSORIES

A few simple items of basic equipment are all your cat needs in order to be a warm, comfortable, and happy member of the household.

PERSONAL PROPERTY

It's not essential to provide your cat with her own bedding and toys, but you can be sure that, if you don't, she will start to improvise by snoozing on your best chair, or by playing with delicate house-plants.

DINNER TIME

A dish for food, with a separate container for water, is vital.

FINE FARE

Uneaten food must not sit around and become stale. Remove any untouched food after half an hour. Wash the bowl thoroughly before the next meal. Place your cat's feeding bowl on newspaper to avoid any mess on the floor.

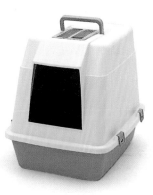

PRIVATE BATHROOM

A hooded litter tray with a carbon-fibre filter to minimize unpleasant odours is the height of feline luxury. Cats appreciate a little privacy, especially in a small or crowded home.

Up to Scratch

If your cat starts to sharpen her claws on the furniture, say "No" firmly. Then carry her over to the scratching post. Attaching a small toy to the post may make it more attractive to feline eyes, and some posts are impregnated with catnip to make them more alluring.

TREATS
FOR YOUR
Cat

*Pamper your feline friend
with very special meals,
body massage, and lots of
fun and games!*

SENSUOUS DELIGHTS

These sublime treats will soon have your cat purring.
Cats enjoy such pleasures as catnip planted in the sun,
or a pot of lush green grass to nibble.

DELECTABLE SCENT
Plant a patch of catnip (*Nepeta cataria*, also called catmint) in a sunny spot. Oils in the leaves contain a chemical component that sends sensitive cats into a state of bliss. Cats roll on the plant, releasing the aroma.

SUCCULENT SNACK
Grass contains valuable vitamins and helps cats to regurgitate hairballs. Chewing grass is not a sign that your cat is ill.

BEDTIME BLISS
Cats like to stretch out, so choose a basket that is big enough. Line it with an old blanket, or, for total luxury, use a lamb's fleece.

BODY MASSAGE
Wait until your cat is on your lap and in the mood for stroking, then begin a gentle "massage". Using both hands, stroke firmly from shoulder to rump, caressing her spine and sides. Then scratch gently behind the ears and on top of the head. Stroke under the chin with your index finger and listen to the purrs!

GOOD COMPANIONS
Human company is vital
to cats. They can
become unhappy and
introverted when they
feel neglected. Consider
taking two kittens from
the same litter, as they
will keep each other
entertained when you
have to go out.

GAMES AND PLAY

Play is a very important part of a cat's life. It's fun –
and cats are devoted to having fun – it's a good way of
getting exercise, and it provides an opportunity
to practise stalking, chasing, and pouncing.
Most cats will play happily on their own,
but are even happier if their owner can
find time for a daily play session.

CATCH AS CAT CAN
*Cats often pounce on
likely looking objects,
just to see if they make
good playthings.*

Good Games
Small objects that can be pulled along, or swung in the air, are ideal for pouncing games. Tweak the bait gently, to alert puss's interest, then just as she's about to pounce, twitch out of reach.

Exercise Time
Bowl a ping-pong ball along the floor, flick pellets of paper into the air, or arrange a newspaper in an upturned "V" to make an inviting hidey-hole.

Favourite Toys
Pet shops offer a wide choice of feline toys, or you can improvise and make your own at home.

Jump for Joy
Any toy scented with catnip will have extra appeal for frisky felines.

TREATS TO EAT

Every cat enjoys a delicious little morsel, prepared specially for feline consumption. While basic cat foods contain all the protein and vitamins needed to sustain your cat, these gourmet treats are guaranteed to tempt the most jaded palate – they are also highly nutritious, and will keep your cat in the absolute peak of condition.

Breakfast Delight

Set your cat off to a great start with a small portion of oat cereal or porridge, made up with milk or a mixture of milk and water. Cool the porridge on a shallow dish, and serve when at room temperature, with an extra teaspoonful of cream on very special occasions.

Sweet Treat

Many health-conscious cats enjoy a little helping of plain yogurt, served just as it is. A thin trickle of honey over the top will be greatly appreciated by some cats. Unflavoured, plain, low-fat yogurt is just as delicious, if your cat is at all inclined to put on weight.

Cheesy Fish Supper

Bake fillets of whiting or coley in foil with a little milk for 15 to 20 minutes. Flake the fish, removing bones. Add the cooking liquid, top with finely grated cheese, and grill lightly. Serve cooled.

Speedy Snack

For a quick, filling meal, mash sardines or pilchards that have been canned in oil. This treat is good for longhaired cats: the oil helps to ease hairballs through the digestive system.

Celebration Feast

Save the turkey giblets, and simmer them gently for about half an hour. Dice the flesh with a few choice pieces trimmed from the bird. Serve moistened with the delicious cooking liquid.

Puss's Pasta

Cook macaroni for 12 minutes until tender. Simmer lean minced beef in a savoury stock for 20 minutes. Combine the mince and macaroni. Cool before serving with grated cheese.

Sublime Soup

For a luscious consommé, simmer meat trimmings and bones in water for an hour, then strain through a fine sieve. A little chopped meat can be added, if liked.

Hearty Beef Stew

Chunks of stewing steak, pressure cooked for 20 minutes in a tasty stock, make a warming supper. Combine the stew with mashed potatoes or rice. Serve when cool.

MENU PLANNING

Cats enjoy a varied diet. Like humans, they get bored
if faced with the same food, day in day out.

CANNED FOOD

Canned pet foods give your cat
all the necessary nutrients,
although you can mix in some
dry biscuits for puss to crunch
on. Do not give dry biscuits on
their own, as they are low in
fat and can cause kidney
problems. An average-sized cat
needs around three-quarters to
a whole can of food per day,
divided into two or three meals.
Keep opened cans covered and
refrigerated. A few seconds in
the microwave brings food up
to an acceptable temperature.
Cats don't enjoy chilled food.

FRESH MEAT AND FISH

Try meals of raw, minced meat (but not pork
or offal, which must *always* be cooked). Pour
savoury juices over the meat before serving.
Don't give liver more than once a week.
Beware of splintery bones in chicken and rabbit.
White or oily fish, lightly cooked, flaked, and
with the bones removed, remains a favourite
feline food. Canned sardines or pilchards are
quick and convenient meals – and highly nutritious.

OTHER PROTEIN FOODS

Hard cheese, grated or diced, and cottage cheese are high in protein. Cooked eggs (scrambled, or hard-boiled and chopped) are ideal for cats, but don't give them raw egg white.

CARBOHYDRATE

If your cat enjoys it, you can stretch a protein meal with bread or cooked rice, pasta or potato. Some cats also like cooked green vegetables, which are useful healthy "fillers".

AND TO DRINK ...

Not all cats like milk and many suffer upset stomachs if they drink it: It is not essential for any cat, once weaned. You should always provide fresh, clean water, although your cat may decide that he prefers puddles, dripping taps, and the contents of flower vases! Some cats dislike the taste of chlorine in tap water, but will happily lap at bottled, still mineral water. Your cat may even appear to drink nothing at all.

Don't worry about this; cats survive happily with very little liquid.

Cat
FACTS

*A treasury of vital
information to enhance
your cat's health
and happiness.*

My Cat's Health and History

My cat's name ....

Date of birth ....

Birthplace ....

Sex ....

Colour of eyes ....

Colour of coat ....

Weight ....

Food favourites and hates ....

....

....

Cat Care Record

Dates of first vaccinations against :

Feline Influenza ....

Feline Infectious Enteritis ....

Annual booster due every ....

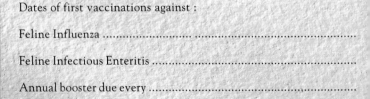

Worming tablets given ....

Birth of first litter ....

Number of kittens ....

Date neutered ....

Name, address, and phone number of vet:

....

....

Dates of visits to the vet, and treatments prescribed:

....

....

....

....

Preferred cat sitters ....

....

....

Preferred catteries ....

....

....

CAT STARS

Cosset your cat according to the stars.

ARIES
21 MARCH – 20 APRIL

Arien cats like to be out and about, tree-climbing and leaf-chasing; they are not pets for flat-dwellers. They have masses of energy and lots of love to give. Keep your Arien female in when she's on heat, as this sign is renowned for its passionate nature.

TAURUS
21 APRIL – 21 MAY

Every evening, on the stroke of feeding time, Taurean cats will be standing impatiently by their bowls. They cling to routine and adore their food. Don't give in to cries for "More". At heart Taureans are country cats that like to roam the fields, chasing butterflies.

GEMINI
22 MAY – 21 JUNE

Although Geminian cats hate being left alone, they don't make very restful companions. Brimming with nervous energy, Geminians jump at the slightest noise and are constantly on the prowl. Then they need lots of sleep, so provide a snug, warm bed.

CANCER
22 JUNE - 22 JULY

Cancerian cats can never get enough affection; they positively adore being stroked and cuddled. Cats born under this sign are very emotional and don't respond well to change or upset. They may suffer from stomach problems, unless life remains calm.

LEO
23 JULY - 23 AUGUST

Keep your wits about you if you own a Leo cat, as this is the daredevil sign that will creep up and steal your supper. Leos are very lovable, though, and are always forgiven. They are happiest in company and adore the companionship of another live-in cat.

VIRGO
24 AUGUST - 22 SEPTEMBER

Simple pleasures of life (fresh fish and a gentle brushing for a treat) make Virgoan cats very happy. They don't like rich food and shun too much fuss. Neat eaters, they spend hours in fastidious washing before curling up contentedly in their tidy beds.

*L*IBRA
23 SEPTEMBER – 23 OCTOBER

Libran cats drive their owners mad with their indecision. Do I want a lap? Or shall I settle on the chair? Would I like some milk? Do I want to come in? Or go out? Librans can never make up their minds, but at heart they truly are comfort-loving cats.

*S*CORPIO
24 OCTOBER – 22 NOVEMBER

Scorpios love rough and tumble and will enjoy strenuous games. They'll even let you rumple their fur, as long as you don't overdo it. Beware the Scorpio cat's jealous nature, and don't be seen fondling another cat unless you want to be ignored for at least a week.

*S*AGITTARIUS
23 NOVEMBER – 21 DECEMBER

Put your best china well out of reach if you own a Sagittarian cat. Despite their natural feline grace and agility, these highly active, boisterous cats can create havoc in the home. Sagittarians are happiest left to roam free, but they always return after their adventures.

Capricorn
22 December – 20 January

Shy of showing their feelings, Capricornians need to be coaxed on to your lap. Once there, they will accept all the love and affection you can give them. They sometimes neglect their appearance, so make sure that longhaired Capricornians are groomed regularly.

Aquarius
21 January – 18 February

You never know what's going to happen next with Aquarian cats. One day they'll follow you around lovingly, the next they won't want to know you at all. Aquarians value their independence intensely, so don't thwart an Aquarian unless it's quite unavoidable.

Pisces
19 February – 20 March

Dreamy Pisceans sit for hours gazing into the fire, lost in a world of their own. They are hypersensitive and hate sudden noises and people with loud voices – anything, in fact, that disturbs their reverie. They are adorable, affectionate pets. And, yes, they love fish.

A-Z of Health and Safety

A IS FOR AGE
Most cats age gracefully, but watch for appetite changes or weight loss, which point to the beginning of health problems.

B IS FOR BREEDING
Keep your pedigree female indoors when on heat. Make arrangements with a breeder for her to be served by a fine recognized male.

C IS FOR CARS
Many cats complain loudly when travelling by car, but in a safe, comfortable basket, no harm will come to them. Carry water, food, and a litter tray on any long journey.

D IS FOR DISEASE
Watch out for warning symptoms such as a cough or cold, sickness, lassitude, or change in appetite.

E IS FOR ELECTRICITY
Cats like to gnaw at flexes and wires. Prevent accidents by unplugging electric appliances when they are not in use.

F IS FOR FIREWORKS
Fun for humans, but terrifying for cats. Keep your cat safely indoors when the pops, bangs, and whizzes begin.

G IS FOR GARAGE
Forbidden territory for cats, who may lick up a puddle of anti-freeze or spilled oil, with disastrous results. Check the garage or garden shed if your cat goes missing. She may have dashed inside when you last opened the door.

H IS FOR HAIRBALLS
Hairballs can become a problem for longhairs, so regular and thorough grooming by you is essential to health.

I IS FOR INJECTIONS

Vaccination in kittenhood and annual boosters protect feline lives.

J IS FOR JITTERS

Nervous cats hate visiting the vet, and can be exceptionally hard to handle. Wrapping the whole body in a towel, leaving the head free, restrains the cat and helps to calm him. Talk reassuringly before, during, and after such restraint.

K IS FOR KITCHEN

A room full of dangers for inquisitive felines. Hotplates, gas burners, and ovens can all give nasty burns. Sharp knives should be kept safely in a drawer beyond paw's reach.

L IS FOR LIPS

If your cat curls back his lips in a grimace, he is showing a feline characteristic known as "flehmen". The cat reacts to exciting scents by pulling this strange, snarling face.

M IS FOR MEDICINES

To administer a pill, hold the cat firmly and grasp the sides of the mouth with your thumb and forefinger. Bend the head back gently and at the same time press the jaws gently so that the mouth opens wide. Drop the pill on to the back of your cat's tongue, then hold her mouth shut until you are quite certain that she has swallowed all her medicine.

N IS FOR NURSING

If your cat does fall ill and needs to be cared for at home, make sure that there is a warm and comfortable bed ready. A hot-water bottle wrapped in a blanket, or a heated pad is always very comforting. Feed a light, tempting diet and do not allow the cat to go out until she has recovered completely. Never give aspirin or paracetamol to a cat that is sick or in pain. It could kill.

O IS FOR OUTDOOR LIFE AND LEISURE

Allow your cat access to the outside world if at all possible. Cats will enjoy the exercise and fresh air, the chance to socialize with other cats, and a snooze in the sun. Nibbling grass is another healthy outdoor pastime.

P IS FOR PARASITES

Infestations of fleas are common, particularly in summer. Treat with a powder or spray.

Q IS FOR QUIET

Cats hate loud noises and hide themselves away from raucous parties or pulsating music. Respect your cat's need for peace and don't force him to endure noise.

R IS FOR REPRODUCTION

Kittens are adorable, but before allowing your cat to produce a litter, be sure that she is in good health. Remember that you will need to find good, caring homes for all the kittens, and be on hand to give several feeds a day when they are very young.

S IS FOR SPAYING

Female cats can have this simple operation any time after the age of four months but not when in season. Spaying involves the removal of both ovaries and much of the uterus under general anaesthetic. It is a very safe, but irreversible operation with no after-effects.

T IS FOR TOILET TRAINING

Introduce kittens to a litter tray when they are three to four weeks of age and beginning to take solid foods. Give the tray a permanent home, somewhere peaceful where the cat can use it undisturbed. Regular cleaning of the litter tray with detergent or baking soda is essential as fastidious cats may refuse to use a soiled tray, and instead will choose a quiet corner in which to perform.

U IS FOR UNIDENTIFIED

A cat without a collar, to which a name tag is securely attached, could stray or be injured with no means for others to alert the worried owner. Most cats quickly adapt to wearing a collar, so make sure your pet never ventures out without one.

V IS FOR VET

Ask local cat-lovers or breeders for the name of a vet who is feline friendly. Choose a reliable practice that works extensively with small animals and that has a 24-hour service in case of emergency. Cats are usually extremely healthy creatures, but a visit is vital for booster vaccinations every year.

W IS FOR WINDOWS

An open window is like a magnet to a curious cat, but even sure-footed felines can fall and injure themselves. Shut your cat out when you want to air upstairs rooms.

X IS FOR XPLORING

It's in a cat's nature to wriggle into any inviting crevice or cranny. Cats can get trapped in drawers, cupboards, garden sheds, washing machines, and freezers, so keep doors securely shut.

Y IS FOR YOLK

Many cats enjoy cooked, chopped egg yolk on other foods as a treat. Give just one or two per week.

Z IS FOR ZAP

What your cat will do to any unwary bird or rodent who crosses her path. If you want a colony of mice wiped out, keep puss well fed. Hungry cats lack the energy needed for serious hunting. Cats bring home prey and offer it as a special gift to their owner. This action is most common in neutered females who have no kittens to instruct in the skill of the chase. Try not to recoil in horror. Praise puss for her generosity – and quietly dispose of the sad remains.

I N D E X

A

accessories 36–37
ageing 56
appetite 56

B

baskets 36, 40
bathroom, private 36
behaviour 14–17
body language 14–17
body massage 40
boosters, annual 57
breeding 56, 58
brushes 29

D

diet 35, 44–47
disease 56
dogs, meeting 24–25

E

ears 14, 17
    cleaning 29, 33
Egyptian cats 10
equipment 36–37
exercise 42–43
expressions 16
eyes 16
    cleaning 29, 33

F

fireworks 56
fleas 23, 30, 58

G

grass 40
grooming 28–33
    longhairs 32–33
    shorthairs 30–31

H

hairballs 40, 56
health record 50–51
hunting 59

I

identity tags 59
injections 22, 57

K

kitten
    bringing home 24–25
    choosing 22–23
    needs 24

L

leads 26
litter tray 27, 36
longhairs 18, 23
    grooming 28–29, 32–33

M

massage 40
medicine, administering 57
menus 46–47
miaowing 16
moods 14–17

N

nervousness 57
neutering 22, 58
noise 16, 58

P

parasites 58
pills, administering 57
play 42–43
prizewinning cats 34–35
purring 14

R

recipes 44–45
recreation 42–43

S

scratching post 37
scent marking 15
shorthairs 18
   grooming 28–31

showing your cat 34–35
spaying 58
star-signs 52–55

T

tail
   communication 14, 16–17
   grooming 32–33
temperament 18–19, 22–23
tooth care 32
toys 43
training 26–27

V

vaccinations 22, 35
vets 59

W

weight loss 56
welcoming gestures 14–15
whiskers 14, 17

ACKNOWLEDGMENTS

Key: t=top; b=bottom.

All photography by Jane Burton except for:
Dave King: 8, 14-15, 17, 23b, 24

Fine Art Photographic Library: 10, 11t
Mary Evans Picture Library: 11b
Animals Unlimited: 12 • Daily Mail: 13t
20th Century Fox: 13b

Design Assistance: Patrizio Semproni, Camilla Fox, Ursula Dawson
Additional Picture Research: Diana Morris
Illustrations: Susan Robertson, Stephen Lings, Clive Spong